The Future Is Ours to Write: 2021

The Future Is Ours to Write: 2021

Edited by Jack Adams, Erik Hvidston, Joshua Parrott, Andrea Skirvin, Chloe Ulmer, & Sarah Snider

Fraternitas Press

The Future Is Ours to Write: 2021

Edited by Jack Adams, Erik Hvidston, Joshua Parrott, Andrea Skirvin, Chloe Ulmer, & Sarah Snider

First Printing, 2021

ISBN: 978-1-7349589-2-8

CONTENTS

CONTENTS

Foreword

Sometimes, you can't help but live in historic, unprecedented times, and that's what we—the Marian University Line Editing Team—faced when we began our journey to become stronger editors. Over the course of four months, our team developed an arsenal of skills to prepare us for the pinnacle of our Line Editing class: the editing and publication of *The Future is Ours to Write: 2021*. All of the time we spent together creating style sheets, proofreading articles, learning the trade of copyediting, and gaining valuable industry knowledge from a host of guest speakers was done while navigating the complications of a pandemic.

Despite the hurdles we faced, we were ready for the project that would become this book. Our professor, Sarah Snider, divided us into two teams and we put our noses to the grindstone. One team oversaw sophomore and junior class essays while the other took on senior class essays and Honorable Mentions. At various stages throughout the editing process, we worked as individuals, partners, and a coherent whole. Collaborating with one another while building our publishing skills through this inspiring project was a highly enriching experience.

This collection of high school essays is a treasure trove of insight and hope for a greater tomorrow. The authors of this book worked exceptionally hard to craft these essays, and their enthusiasm in working with our team to see their writing published was perhaps the most rewarding part of this whole process. This book, and the writings within, will impact the Indianapolis community by showing that younger generations are not merely dismayed by the current pandemic, but hopeful of a more prosperous and humanitarian world.

—The Marian University Line Editing Team
Spring 2021

Introduction

The Future is Ours to Write is a project created by the Marian University Department of English inviting students in grades 9-12 to submit essays on creative solutions for challenges inhibiting a positive future. The essay contest that sparked the publication of this book recognized the progressive ideas of students' visions of a new future. Dealing with topics spanning from mental health struggles to racial issues, these essays have painted a positive outlook for the world. The inclusion of their personal narratives has allowed the writers to appeal to the experiences of a wide audience given that everybody is currently struggling with a global pandemic and understanding social injustices within our society.

As members of the Marian University Line Editing Team, we were inspired by the level of creativity and ingenuity exhibited by these high school writers. Our experiences with these essays have brought us hope and excitement for the leaders of tomorrow, while also giving us the chance to understand the strife of newer generations during this time. The opportunity to edit and develop young writers' thoughts into the best version of their narratives has given us a platform to connect with and share their unique perspectives on the world's issues. This book inspires its readers to consider different ways that we as a society might think or act towards the significant issues that we deal with on a daily basis. As editors, we were able to sense the ambition and drive empowering these students to make a difference in the world.

We were encouraged by the depth and intelligence of the essays as they relate to problems that affect all of our communities. The writers' meticulous analysis of their surroundings is bound to transform the world as we know it. Although these students are still young, due to living through a global pandemic, a climate crisis, and ongoing struggles with racial injustice, they have been subject to some of the same trials and tribulations that would have previously only come with age. These students will become our future, and as a collective group they have crafted essays that bring a progressive outlook on what lies ahead for our society.

How Was Your Day?

"Hello, Nico Rivera. Please rate how you feel today out of 10. With 10 feeling overly exuberant, having rapid thoughts, and detaching from reality. And 1 feeling a lack of energy, experiencing suicidal thoughts, or confused thinking."

Nico's eyes linger on the computer speakers and skim the screen. He goes through the same processes as 76 million children in the United States. Free AI therapy sessions were declared mandatory in 2034 for every child between the ages of 5 and 18. The automatic system knows to wait two minutes for a response before asking a follow-up question.

Nico scuffs his Chuck Taylor's on the carpeted floor, twiddling with his nails and rocking on the edge of his seat. He waits until he can't take the silence anymore after 1 minute and 55 seconds. "Three," he breaths out. Letting out all of the air he has held in all day, all week. The small room swallows him whole. Escaping the folding walls, Nico abruptly stands up, walking aimlessly back and forth, passing dirty clothes and crumpled paper on the floor. The navy-blue blinds conceal the light, leaving the room dark on a sunny Saturday.

"Nico, take a deep breath," the AI states.

He pauses.

"Why are you feeling stressed?"

"Safari, we are human; therefore, we all have problems," he says, trying to will a smile on his face. The AI (Safari) can see past the fake efforts.

"I don't know, I'm stressed, I have college applications to fill out. I still don't know what I want to do with my life," he states, picking up a book to distract himself. His shoulders hunch over and the words spill out of his mouth. "I feel alone, okay. I feel like no one cares about me. I feel like I just watch time go by, and I can't react because I am numb. Numb to it all. I can't think about my future if I can't get through today," he whispers.

Poor mental health is a global crisis that will only increase as social inequities progress. According to NAMI (National Alliance on Mental Illness), 1 out of 5 children in the U.S is living with a mental health condition. In 2015, 17% of high school students were seriously considering suicide (Pane). 50% of children between the ages of 8-15 who are experiencing a mental health condition didn't receive treatment (NAMI). Today, we can promote awareness and create innovative solutions focusing on preventable measures, so in the future we have resources to combat the mental health crisis.

The Diagnostic and Statistical Manual of Mental Disorders (DSM) defines mental illness as "a behavioral or psychological syndrome or pattern that occurs in an individual," while mental health refers to "cognitive, behavioral, and emotional well-being" (U.S. Department of Health & Human Services). Although mental health and mental illnesses are related, they are separate.

Someone could have great mental health but have a mental illness.

There is not one innovative solution that will solve the pain and suffering of someone who experiences mental health problems. It will take everyone coming together as a community to create a better world. All social justice issues are interconnected, intricately interwoven like a spiderweb. Therefore, we can't just focus on mental health. We must focus on poverty, racial inequality, the criminal justice system, homelessness, immigration, the climate crisis, addiction, and abuse. Marginalized communities are less likely to reach out for mental health services although they are impacted the most.

Complex issues need to be approached with complex solutions. I propose an increase in funding for schools to support students' mental health by providing an increase in counseling services and more training in schools. First responders should be provided with more training on how to deal with people in distress. We need to have more wrap-around services like centers for community members to access help with finding jobs and housing. Raising the minimum wage to a livable wage will decrease stress and anxiety for those living in poverty. The cost of health care is often a barrier, with millions of Americans having to choose between running water or medication. We can eliminate that choice and make health care affordable for all; we can do anything we put our mind to. Radical change starts with small steps.

You can take the first step today by talking with your friends and family about mental health. By having open dialogue with your community on how we can help each other and the world.

Youth are not just the future leaders of tomorrow; we are the leaders of today.

A week later, Nico sits 38,000 feet above the ground.

"Welcome to World Airlines, thank you for flying. We just have a few announcements for you today. Please be cautious of your trash consumption. Save all recyclable or reusable items for the end of the flight and place them in the upcycle station on the left of the door when we land. Please look under your seats and take notice of the HT Human Trafficking button. If pressed, assistance will be provided." The scratchy intercom calms the masses.

The first hour of the flight goes by smoothly. Nico reads an old classic, The Hunger Games. *On the plane, everyone's heads are bowed as bright lights illuminate their faces. Countless people try to feel less alone in crowded rows. Nico notices a small girl sitting next to a large man near the back of the plane. The girl's hands are trembling, but from what he can see of her face, she is emotionless. She wears sunglasses, a hat, and a baggy sweatshirt. The man holds her knee possessively.*

Nico knows something is wrong. Looking under his seat, he presses the bright red button. Once the flight is landed, the authorities stop the girl and the man. As Nico walks past the blond girl, tears stream down her red face as she looks away, silently thanking Nico. He makes his way through the crowded airport. A yellow cab with solar panels on top pulls up in front of him. Jumping into the back seat, he types his mother's address into the customer tablet and the driverless car drives away.

The car pulls into a driveway of a small cottage house with white trims and a green mailbox. It is a typical November day in Texas, hot and humid. Nico prefers Indiana's unpredictable weather.

The front door bursts open. "Nico baby!" His mother embraces him in a hug.

"I'm fine, Mom, let's just go inside. How is Rocky doing?"

"Besides tearing up my furniture, fine," she replies, laughing.

Standing in the modern chic kitchen, Nico shakes his head; the house hasn't changed at all. It is still as barren and boring as before. All the pictures are still a snapshot of ten years ago.

"How is your father doing?" she asks, tidying up the already clean house.

"Good, he has been taking more shifts. Still writing about how the aliens are coming, and of course, how could I forget, he joined a VR baseball team," he says, petting Rocky.

His mother stares out the window, reminiscing.

"Have you been on top of your EW (emotional wellness) sessions?" His mother doesn't need to ask this question. If a student misses a single session, a call will go straight to their parents and the school.

The sun is starting to set. Nico pulls out his laptop and sits at his desk.

"Hello, Nico Rivera. How are you? Please rate how you feel today."

Works Cited

American Psychiatric Association. "Diagnostic and Statistical Manual of Mental Disorders (DSM–5)." *DSM-5*, 2013, www.psychiatry.org/psychiatrists/practice/dsm.

NAMI. "Mental Health Facts in America." *National Alliance on Mental Illness*, 2021, www.nami.org/nami/media/nami-media/infographics/generalmhfacts.pdf.

Pane, Natalia E. "The Rate of High School-Aged Youth Considering and Committing Suicide Continues to Rise, Particularly among Female Students." *Child Trends*, 27 Apr. 2020, www.childtrends.org/blog/high-school-aged-youth-considering-and-committing-suicide-among-female-students.

Sohn, Emily. "Can Poverty Lead to Mental Illness?" *NPR*, NPR, 30 Oct. 2016, www.npr.org/sections/goatsandsoda/2016/10/30/499777541/can-poverty-lead-to-mental-illness.

U.S. Department of Health & Human Services. "What Is Mental Health?" *MentalHealth.gov*, 28 May 2020, www.mental-health. gov/basics/what-is-mental-health.

The Time for Change Is Now

The year 2020 took a huge turn three to four weeks into the year. Many people know that we lost a legend and his daughter, Kobe and GiGi Bryant, may they rest in peace. We thought that it couldn't get any worse, but it did. We were all hit with a worldwide pandemic which has taken a toll on the lives of not just Americans, but those around the world. Then came the death of George Floyd, which was the start to ongoing protest and fights for justice. Let's not forget about the rioting and looting as well, which seems to be a very common thing that happens when Americans feel like they aren't being heard or they don't like the way things are going. It reminds me of the rioting that took place in the 1700s because the people were being taxed without representation. It amazes me how some things never change. But besides that, this is all taking place during a pandemic. At this point in the year, I feel a huge separation within our country. Some people are agreeing to wearing masks and some refuse. Some support the Black Lives Matter movement, and some don't. And that's what I want to talk about—the Black Lives Matter movement and how it's affected me and what I want to do to change it.

As a little girl I moved around a lot, which meant every year I was at a different school. Those schools were always made up of predominantly Black students. I had even gone to a school with predominantly Hispanic students before. So, I wasn't really aware of how real racism was or how discrimination was a thing. But then I moved to a predominantly white area my fourth-grade year, and that's when I knew. I was one of three black girls at my school and it was definitely different. None of the girls, besides the Black ones, wanted to be my friend at first and I wasn't sure why. As I got older, I discovered why and now that I think about it, that's a sad thing for a nine-year-old to experience. I remember learning about the Declaration of Independence during my years in elementary and the commonly used phrase, "All men are created equal." If that was true, why didn't I feel equal to my peers in class? Why did it seem like we weren't equal?

Fast forward seven years, the year is 2020, and now I've had a couple of personal situations with racism. In one of them I was actually called the N word with a hard R. I tell you, that took a toll on my life and how I see people. Now, with the BLM movement taking place, my perspective has changed even more. I 100% understand people not supporting the rioting and looting; why should they? But not supporting the BLM movement at all, and not only that but making a phrase, "All Lives Matter" in opposition of the movement? As if we don't understand that all lives matter? Because we do, but all lives can't matter until Black lives do. And to see how those two phrases have torn this country apart is saddening.

But I feel like we can be brought back together if we all just try. I know that is definitely easier said than done and it also sounds like a very basic statement. But maybe if we stop trying to degrade and bash each other over our differences and decide to hear each other out and listen for valid points, maybe then we can bring this country together. If we spread more love and less hate, maybe then we could bring this country back together. If we stop standing against each other, put our differences aside, and stand with each other. Martin Luther King Jr. made a change for generations after him, and that's what I want to do. But I know that if I want it to happen it has to start with me.

I plan on spreading love regardless of your race, beliefs, or even political views. Some people don't understand that you don't have to agree with everything someone does to be able to be friends with them. And if we all start being kind to each other, maybe we can get kindness to spread as much as the hate does. Although I don't control what takes place in other people's home, I do control what takes place in mine, and I choose to teach love. It all starts at home. We have to start teaching the next generations love and we have to stop teaching discrimination, racism, and inequality. Such a small thing could take our country a long way.

Quarantine and Its Effects on Mental Health

When we first entered the year 2020, we never thought that the year would be so disastrous. From Australia being on fire to the murder hornets, the universe really seemed to hate us. But despite all of these problems that we have faced, maybe they have actually helped us take a clearer look into our society. This pandemic that we have faced has really opened our eyes to the world around us, despite ironically having to be stuck inside. We can take a look into the Coronavirus pandemic and see how it has affected us as of now and how it can better improve our mental health for the future through the shared experience of hardship, family, and new interests.

When we first said that we were going back to the roaring 20s with the year 2020, we never thought that we were going to experience its hardships as well as a pandemic, and even an economic depression following suit. Out of all of the deaths of loved ones and having to make changes in our lives to help protect ourselves and others against the virus, many may assume that we have reached the lowest point of our lives, but that's far from the truth. The quarantine seems to have created some more remarkable changes to ourselves and how we have behaved besides just being stressful. Quarantine has given us time to reflect and try new things which ended up actually bettering our mental health. Through this shared experience of living through a pandemic, we can now relate to each other more than ever. We have all experienced fearing for our loved ones and each other during this pandemic. Fearing that someone you know has tested positive for COVID. But this is an experience that everyone can connect to now, and that most of us find ways to make light of despite how grim it is. Shared experiences often help us connect to one another on an emotional level, and maybe this is a good thing.

For me, the pandemic wasn't that stressful. Most of my days were just getting up to do my school work for the day and then relax, that was it. I had to admit it was difficult to not be in the traditional school setting, but there was a brighter side to things. Being made to stay inside opened my eyes, and I got a chance to spend more time with my mom. Before, I never really had the time to hang out with my mom; we were both busy, me with school and my mom with work. We only got to see each other in the mornings before we left and, in the afternoons, when we got home. Even though quarantine was hard to go through, at least we have our family. In this day and age, we have been losing touch with our family and friends. Usually, we are so busy with our everyday lives, such as work or going on social media, that we never hang out anymore. Quarantine has given many the chance to reconnect with family and to spend time that they had never really had before with them. Our families are our support system; without them we would struggle with our day to day lives, unsure of what to do next. This quarantine has helped us all make the bond between families stronger. It's like they say, the only way you can get family together is locking them in a room.

The twenty-first century brought a rise to technology which, even though it was intended to serve a purpose to connect us to the farthest reaches of the world, instead created a gap between each other. We should take this quarantine into account to help make us better as human beings. For the first time in a long time, we have begun to put down our phones and start trying new things in a limited space. During quarantine, many people undertook learning new skills, such as reading a book or even baking bread. Technology has stressed us to the point where it is hard for us to even cope without it. The boredom that had risen out of quarantine introduced us to new things outside of the screens of our phones. It gave us time to be creative and explore new interests. It is important to have hobbies since they are a good way to cope with stress. The quarantine gave many the chance to find out what interests them and help them discover new things to love.

Our world is constantly changing in both a good and bad way. But as the next generation who is set to make a change in this world, perhaps we should rearrange our thinking on how to make the world a better place. We take so much time out of our lives to work on things for society that, maybe, we should take a break ourselves. The best way to make a change in the world is to begin with yourself. By bettering our mental health, we can make better and clearer choices for the future. We can't do anything for the world if we are not in the right mental mindset.

The Existential Threat to Humanity

According to the Intergovernmental Panel on Climate Change (IPCC), one of the most prominent scientific assessors of climate change, the "warming of the climate system is unequivocal," and the changes in weather patterns and temperature seen as a result of this are "unprecedented" (Denchak). These changes, as posited by 97% of climate scientists, are largely as a result of the actions of people. In order to combat this man-made ordeal, many reports are finding that we have to drastically reduce carbon dioxide emissions by 2030. We must also have net-zero emissions, meaning as many carbon emissions have been absorbed as released, by 2075. This issue of climate change will affect every person on the planet if nothing more is done. Because of this, every person, every city, and every country must do everything they can to reduce greenhouse gas emissions. Individual people need to convert to energy-efficient appliances and vehicles. Cities need to make cleaner travel easier. Nations need to act on legislation similar to the ever-popular Green New Deal.

Every person must understand that they contribute to the worsening of climate change. To minimize said crisis, simply switching to a clean refrigerator, a hybrid or electric car, and other clean energy options can drastically reduce a person's carbon footprint. Using electric or hybrid cars, along with using energy-efficient appliances, would do just that. After energy-use standards were implemented in 1987 for these appliances, the standards "have kept 2.3 billion tons of carbon dioxide out of the air" (Denchak). Using appliances with an "Energy Star" label has prevented emissions equal to the annual emissions of 440 million cars. Hybrid cars can lower the amount of pollution from cars as well. Given the high number of miles per gallon of fuel in a hybrid car, they "cut...automotive emissions by half" (Denchak). These are massive amounts of carbon dioxide emissions. The massive amount of emissions can be substantially lessened, and as a result, the effects of the emissions will follow suit. All that needs to be done is a conversion to clean energy. Despite the common claim that green cars and appliances are more expensive than those that are not, in reality, the opposite is true. Hybrid cars get nearly double the miles per gallon of the average car. This change not only could save the planet, but also save Americans $80 billion a year (Denchak). If people took these small steps, emissions of greenhouse gasses would be significantly lessened.

Cities—and the planning of these cities—also play an enormous role in attempting to reduce carbon emissions. Cities need to readjust in order to accommodate green transportation. Adjustments can include making cities more compact and walkable, while also encouraging electric and hybrid cars, and public transportation. Transportation in cities is "the second highest source" of urban greenhouse gas emissions (Race). To solve this glaring problem, cities need to be planned in a more compact, centralized fashion, as "Walking or biking could substitute for 41 percent of short car trips, saving nearly 5 percent of carbon dioxide emissions from car travel" (Atherton). As illustrated, hybrid and electric cars also come with many benefits for both the environment and the pocketbook. City leaders need to encourage residents to make this transition to low-emission travel in order to achieve the best results. While such changes may seem drastic, the reality is that many cities have applied these solutions and found positive results. Cities and the actions that they take will play a critical part in the fight to reduce carbon emissions and minimize the effects of climate change. It is integral that they do all that they can.

Nations around the world have perhaps the biggest responsibility to act. They have the ability to do more than any one person or city. Because they can do so much to combat climate change and lower carbon emissions, they must. These big steps that they can take come in the form of the Green New Deal. This proposal calls for a "10-year mobilization," which would handily meet the goal of net-zero emissions by 2050 (Prakash). Net-zero emissions would be obtained following ambitious goals, including transitioning "100 percent of our electricity generation to renewable sources" and "invest[ing] in projects to capture climate-damaging gases already in the atmosphere" (Prakash). This plan would meet lofty climate goals all while creating nearly 30 million jobs. Some people, especially those who have jobs in the fossil fuel industry, would inevitably lose their jobs. Despite this harsh reality, if the Green New Deal is followed, the government would provide the training for these people to be trained in a clean energy job rather than one that is not so. The Green New

Deal, in defiance of its being the pathway to a cleaner Earth and stronger economy, has developed a strong opposition. Such critics will often claim that the deal is too radical, too expensive, and too much in too little time. While it is certainly true that the Green New Deal has demanding goals and requires decisive action, the fact remains that the climate crisis is not something that can be ignored or set aside because it would be too difficult to fight it. Even so, there are many less demanding plans—albeit riskier in regard to the climate—that have been proposed. For instance, 2020 United States presidential candidate Joe Biden has introduced his "Clean Energy Revolution." Biden's plan attempts to do many of the same things as the Green New Deal, though more slowly. It would have total clean energy reliance by 2050, leaving little room for error (Garcia-Navarro). Either way, it is absolutely vital to the future of this planet that nations around the world resolve to meet high objectives to lower carbon emissions.

In the last year, carbon dioxide emissions have risen by 2.7% globally (Friedman). Swift and decisive action must be taken by 2030 in order to avoid a "catastrophic" rise of temperatures by two degrees Celsius (Washington Post Opinions Staff). This action will look like conversion to cleaner energy on the part of individuals, facilitation of green transportation on the part of urban communities, and thorough, ambitious plans from countries around the world to achieve net-zero emissions. While it is absolutely imperative that these things are done, perhaps the most important thing that a person can do is to speak up. Climate change is an issue that will grip our planet for generations to come, which is what makes it so disappointing that too many of our leaders are unwilling to acknowledge that it even exists. Every person must call representatives into action, donate to organizations that are fighting for these solutions, and most importantly, vote. Everyone must vote for someone who will follow science to ensure the future of Planet Earth.

Works Cited

Brady, Jeff, et al. "Breaking Down Joe Biden's Plan To Make the US Carbon Neutral." NPR, 25 Oct. 2020, https://www.npr.org/2020/10/25/927564427/breaking-down-joebidens-plan-to-make-the-u-s-carbon-neutral. Accessed 30 Oct. 2020.

Denchak, Melissa. "Global Climate Change: What You Need to Know." NRDC, 23 2 2017, https://www.nrdc.org/stories/global-climate-change-what-you-need-know. Accessed 30 Oct. 2020.

Denchak, Melissa. "How You Can Stop Global Warming." NRDC, 17 July 2017, https://www.nrdc.org/stories/how-you-can-stop-global-warming. Accessed 22 Oct. 2020.

Friedman, Lisa. "What is the Green New Deal? A Climate Proposal, Explained." New York Times, 21 2 2019, https://www.nytimes.com/2019/02/21/climate/green-new-dealquestions-answers.html. Accessed 30 Oct. 2020.

Post Opinions Staff. "Opinion: Here Are 11 Climate Change Policies to Fight for in 2019." The Washington Post, WP Company, 2 Jan. 2019, www.washingtonpost.com/news/opinions/wp /2019/01/02/feature/opinion-here-are-11-climate-change-policies-to-fight-for-in-2019/. Accessed 30 Oct. 2020.

Race, Bruce. "Climate Change and Cities: What We Need to Do." Forbes, 15 10 2018, https://www.forbes.com/sites/uhenergy/2018/10/15/climate-change-and-cities-what-we-need-to-do/#2267be6c28f6. Accessed 30 Oct. 2020.

Andrew J. Haddock

The Undiscussed Hardship of Immigrant Life in a Systemically Racist America and a Second-Generation Immigrant's Solution on Bettering Such

In a political climate where the lives of immigrants fleeing violence are unvalued and manipulated for political gain, there is a desperate need to amplify their cries and work against the sheltering of Americans' perceptions of the troubles the common immigrant endures under the current American administrations such as Immigration and Customs Enforcement (ICE) and Customs and Border Protection (CBP). I strongly believe massive reform must be done on a federal level to put an end to incessant violence and hardship towards immigrants in the United States. What must be discussed is how we, as the American people, can make the lives of immigrants seeking safety within our border easier, more opportune, equal, and understood.

Firstly, before analyzing solutions to an undiscussed problem, you must understand what the problems are. In today's America, there is a question that is asked most frequently when the topic of immigration is discussed: "Why don't they just do it legally?" There are many answers to this complicated question. First off, while many presidencies and administrations are to blame for corruption amidst our immigration system, the Trump administration has the highest level of this blame. The primary answer to said question would be because our country is making legal entry nearly impossible. The majority of illegal immigrants in our country are not the people rightfully seeking refuge across the southern border, but rather people who are guilty of visa overstay, meaning their visas have expired and they are no longer in the United States legally. A few examples of the many instances our country has made the legal pathway of immigration harder include seeking asylum at a price rather than for free, applying within a quantitative capacity and through a limited number of means and causes. Seeking asylum is asking for granted legal access into the country as an escape from a fear of or already occurred persecution in their country of origin regarding their own race, religion, political opinion, nationality, or membership in a particular social group. In countries such as the one my mother was born in (Honduras), you often have three choices in life: You must flee the country illegally, become a soldier whilst a mere child, or join a gang, where you are then the predator rather than those who are frequently preyed upon. This means of passage has been corrupted and skewed to encourage unrightful deportation and an increase in the number of detainees present within facilities overflowing with accusations of sexual assault, neglect, battery, and more. For example, many asylum seekers are "like Berta, a woman featured in the Netflix documentary *Immigration Nation*, who fled Honduras after MS-13 gang members threatened to light her on fire and force her 12-year-old granddaughter into marriage. Berta turned herself into US authorities at the border as she claimed asylum, only to be separated from her granddaughter and held indefinitely in a US detention center" (Horton). There are countless reasons, examples, and instances of cruelty, neglect, abuse, and manipulation towards the immigrants coming into our country all because legal entry into the United States takes up to many years and even decades before you're even considered, which is an amount of time people in fear for their life simply can't and don't afford. In these detention centers, authorities abuse the detainees who are infested with lice, infected with the flu, suffering from deteriorating dental health, and fearing rape and sterilization thereafter.

Now that you, the reader, are aware of a mere droplet of the problems within our immigration system, we must look at opportunities to better the lives of those seeking refuge by granting them what every human should have—a right to life, liberty, and the pursuit of happiness. To solve these issues ingrained within our immigration systems, I firmly believe we should do away with these systems as a whole and start anew, policies and all. ICE and CBP have not been around forever. These agencies are fairly new, being created under the Bush administration on March 1, 2003 ("History of ICE"; "CBP is Born"). To put it into perspective, both administrations are younger than the average high school senior.

There are too many people stripped of their rights on their deathbed for our country's current process to be deemed anything but cruel and unsatisfactory. The primary reason why reform isn't a thing of the present is because the cruelty being inflicted upon these desperate people is being enforced by the government branches themselves. This is one of the main reasons people dislike our current political composition when it comes to the Senate (legislative), the President (executive), and now the Supreme Court (judicial) in light of recent events regarding the replacement of the late Justice Ruth Bader Ginsburg. This is the main reason why reform must be done from the top, altering who has the highest status, salary, power, and people at their disposal for political gain. In order to make the lives of immigrants easier, we must first make the immigration process in its entirety more practical, based, and welcoming on both sides of the border. We must fight and vote for a presidency and Senate who value the life of the immigrant rather than the monetary value they hold. They do this as a means of "kissing up" to someone of high status by looking unwavering, lawful, and protective of their home, the United States, or expressing racially-motivated views they may hold through their actions and proposals. We must make the legal process easier by overturning bigoted procedures and starting anew with new laws, new proposals, and new requirements to be granted legal access in a country where you are in a drastically safer environment when worrying about murder, gang violence, rape, torture, etc.

In order to do these things, and vote out those who are manipulative and serve themselves rather than the country they swore to represent and fight for, we must educate the American people and give them reasons for these pleas of reform, rather than leave them in the dark when discussing issues such as this. As a country, we see illegal immigrants under these administrations as rapists, criminals, drug smugglers, and terrorists when they are in fact the very people escaping others who perpetuate these crimes.

In closing, we as people, not political powers, must value the life of immigrants and educate, enforce, and demand that the cruelty inflicted on them and their families be stopped. Drastic reform and replacement of our current agencies in control of America's immigration process is necessary in order to make their lives easier, more opportunity-filled, equal, and understood.

Works Cited

"March 1, 2003: CBP is Born." *U.S. Customs and Border Protection,* Updated 1 August 2016, https://www.cbp.gov/about/ history/march-1-2003-cbp-born. Accessed 25 March 2021.

"History of ICE." *U.S. Immigration and Customs Enforcement,* Updated 29 Jan. 2021, https://www.ice.gov/history. Accessed 25 March 2021.

Horton, Adrian. "John Oliver on Trump Immigration policies: 'Truly disciplined about being truly evil'." *The Guardian,* 26 Oct. 2020. www.theguardian.com/culture/2020/oct/26/ john-oliver-trump-immigration-last-week-tonight-recap. Accessed 1 Nov. 2020.

Vacant Stares

In the United States, only twenty-eight states have mandatory sex education, and in those states, the topics of rape and consent are "not required" in the curriculum (Johnson & Bradford). One in every five women in the US will become a victim of sexual assault (RAINN), whereas, in countries like Japan, where rape education is implemented in schools, only one in every twenty women will be sexually assaulted in their lifetime. Japan isn't the only country seeing the positive effects of rape education. In Italy, Singapore, and Greece, where schools have implemented some form of consent training and the countries have enforced strict laws against rape, the rate of rapes is nearly twenty percent less than it is in the United States (World Population Review). From these numbers, a solution to America's epidemic of rape is presented. Some form of rape education needs to be implemented in schools.

While this solution is achievable, there are many barriers society has to overcome before rape education can become an American reality. The first issue in American society is the widely shared belief that the victim "asked for it" in the way they dressed or held themselves. This idea is a big part of rape culture. On the Marshall University Women's Center webpage, rape culture is defined as "an environment in which sexual violence against women is normalized and excused in the media and popular culture." While rape culture is not unique to the US, it has become a big reason why rapists are rarely prosecuted, and why ninety-one percent of rapes go unreported. Societal victim-blaming is fueled by the notion that rape prevention is learning how not to get raped instead of how to ask for consent. With rape education in schools, questions about rape can be steered away from victim-blaming and directed towards not becoming a perpetrator.

For future victims and possible perpetrators, the presented solution has no negative consequences. According to *edweek.org*, where rape education has been provided, "rape rates have decreased by half." Rape education is basic health, so the curriculum could be added to any form of health class with no extra cost to the school or taxpayers. Implementation of this education also allows tough questions about rape to have a uniform answer. This could provide clarity on the definition of consent, sexual assault, and rape, and go as far as how to report misconduct and assault. The topic of rape is considered taboo for the reason that nobody wants to talk about such an unthinkable act. But the twenty percent of women who will be raped in America don't have the choice to just push it under the rug. For so many women that are living with heavy hearts being victimized has left them with a harsh reality. With the implementation of rape education, the topic of rape can move from being taboo to being encouraging and allow compassion for survivors and their stories.

Rape may seem like an inconsequential issue to anyone who is not a young woman, but rape has no boundaries. While the majority of victims are women between the ages of sixteen to twenty-four, one in every ten men will become a victim of sexual assault (Arzate). These numbers include your loved ones, your peers, and the people around you that you may not know. Preventing rape is not the only goal of rape education. Considering that "one in three men would rape if they knew they'd get away with it" according to *wearawhitefeather.wordpress.com*, rape education is intended to teach consent in order to steer men away from becoming a perpetrator, not just teach women how to avoid becoming a victim. With the newer generations, you see more acceptance for survivors and the encouragement for self-education. While this is the first step to a better life for victims of assault, it isn't enough of a preventative measure for the future.

Less than a month ago, a peer of mine had their name added to the never-ending list of survivors and got their dignity stolen from them. At just fifteen, she had to go through what twenty percent of women experience in today's America. "Every 73 seconds an American is sexually assaulted", according to *rainn.org*. Considering my age and gender, I am at high risk. The hard truth is that many of my peers have already faced an assault, and any of your daughters, sisters, or friends could become a victim at any moment. If the presented solution is put into effect, the national number of rapes will go down, the toxicity surrounding rape culture will be diminished, and the people you care most about will be less at risk. For now, all society can do is educate themselves and the people around them. Until the people of the US win the fight for rape education, men and women everywhere are at risk for assault.

Works Cited

Arzate, Héctor Alejandro. "Why the Increase in Sexual Assaults Reported by Schools?" *Education Week*, Education Week, 30 July 2019, www.edweek.org/leadership/why-the-increase-in-sexual-assaults-reported-by-schools/2019/07.

Johnson, Tahra, and Kate Bradford. *State Policies on Sex Education in Schools*, www.ncsl.org/research/health/state-policies-on-sex-education-in-schools.aspx.

Marshall University. "Rape Culture." *Womens Center*, 2021, www.marshall.edu/wcenter/sexual-assault/rape-culture/.

Osaki, Tomohiro. "Fight against Sexual Abuse in Japan Gains Strength." *The Japan Times*, 14 July 2020, www.japantimes.co.jp/news/2020/07/14/national/social-issues/sex-crimes-violence/.

The Order of the White Feather. "Blog." *The Order of the White Feather*, wearawhitefeather.wordpress.com/blog/.

RAINN. "Victims of Sexual Violence: Statistics." *RAINN*, 2020, www.rainn.org/statistics/ victims-sexual-violence.

Rape Statistics by Country 2021, 2021, worldpopulationreview.com/country-rankings/rape-statistics-by-country.

A Future for the Kind

People often say that hardships are meant to toughen you up. The more you endure, the colder you become. You wrap yourself in armor and lock up all the doors, so maybe the next time life throws stones they'll bounce off instead of bruising. This perspective has its merits; it would be wonderful if after every struggle, you were better insulated against the next. But it's also a very lonely way to live. We can only put up so many layers of defenses before they smother us. What if, instead of letting 2020 drown us in waves upon waves of mourning veils and fire retardant and n-95s and boarded up windows, we chose to fling the doors open? What if we chose kindness and warmth over paranoia and frigidity? What could that look like?

At 11:59 pm on December 31st, 2020, most of the world collectively resolves to leave the discord and divisiveness of 2020 in the past. The COVID pandemic surged again over the winter, once again forcing the world inside. But by January 1st, numbers have begun to decline. This spike was different from the first; there were more cases, but fewer deaths. This is attributed to the overwhelming support given to healthcare workers. Gone were the empty platitudes of the first wave- the wealthy and influential put their money where their mouths were and bought enough PPE to protect every hospital worker who needed it. Governments across the globe converted empty hotels to apartment buildings for those who needed shelter, and clothing companies set to work making masks to be delivered on doorsteps, free of charge for everyone who needed it. Even as numbers declined, people kept their mouths and noses covered, not out of fear for themselves but instead out of a desire to protect their neighbors. We washed our hands and kept sanitizer in our purses for ourselves, yes, but for strangers too. Cases were traced quickly and effectively, and government programs covered all hospitalization costs for victims of the pandemic. The economy, surprisingly, boosted instead of falling. Citizens supported small businesses in their time of need, and CEOs took pay cuts so their workers could put food on the table. By the new year, cases in your state were contained enough that you could spend an afternoon with your grandmother, and hug her before you left.

By December of this year, citizens of the US and beyond realized that the protests and riots over the death of George Floyd and so many others weren't perpetuated out of a desire to cause violence, but rather a desire to be heard. After countless petitions reached over a million signatures, the officers responsible for the unjustifiable murders of black people were fired and jailed. The families of their victims could feel peace at last. Legislators in states across the country listened to the voices of their constituents, and began the long and arduous process of creating civil programs designed to truly protect rather than intimidate. Across the nation, offices began popping up for civil servants who responded to nonviolent emergency calls. Each and every one of them was trained in psychology and mediation techniques. Rates of violence in communities began to drop, and citizens in previously over-policed neighborhoods slowly started to trust the system. They could have faith that the officers who protected their city were truly there to keep them safe. All the hurt and anguish felt by the black community over centuries of oppression could not be erased or undone, but at last, real changes were being made.

The wildfires on the west coast left countless Americans homeless, helpless, and hopeless. States as far away as New York dispatched firefighters to help tame the blaze, and when the last ember was extinguished, architects came from all around to begin the process of rebuilding. Meanwhile, those lucky enough to have been spared by the blazes took in their neighbors. They knew they couldn't return what the fire stole, but at the very least they could offer comforting warmth instead of raging heat. California's leadership and that of its neighboring states realized the wildfire season would only get worse if something wasn't done. They conferred with leaders of the indigenous peoples who had tended to the land for decades, and came up with plans for controlled burns to prevent future devastation. Leaders and constituents alike finally opened their eyes to the realities of our ever-changing climate, and resolved to do something about it while they still could. The year 2021 saw a sharp drop off in the use of natural gases and petroleum for power, and an uptick in cities and towns switching to solar and hydroelectric power. The United States rejoined the Paris Accords, and emissions were decreased more than anyone thought possible. Ice in the Antarctic began to reform, and the globe worked together to pull ourselves back from the brink of climate disaster. The west coast is hopeful they'll never see another wildfire season like the one in 2020.

The world I have envisioned here is not perfectly kind or good. It is not the likely scenario, or even really a possible scenario. I acknowledge the bleakness of our current state, the inherent cruelty that accompanies humanity, and that I may not fully understand enough economic principles to accurately predict the trends I'd like to think could occur. But I also acknowledge that no plague can last forever, beside that inherent cruelty rests inherent kindness, and I can always take an economics class in college if I want to understand better. There is no limit to humanity's potential for both good and bad. It would be ignorant of me to claim good is always the easiest choice. Sometimes hope must be fought for, kindness must come from a place of great pain. Hurting and strife is guaranteed, happiness in the face of it all is not. The way it seems to me, everyone has two choices; you can either build walls to hide from the pain, or you can go out and fight it with all you have. 2020 has taught me that I would rather fight and end up with some scars than hide and survive unscathed. What will you choose?

Homelessness: The Obstacle of Understanding

I am a city girl. I have grown accustomed to and almost savor the "normal" city behaviors such as busy lines at coffee shops, business people walking around in high heels and suits, and ethnic cuisine restaurants on every street. I have also, like many city girls, witnessed homelessness and rarely thought twice about the person with a blanket laying on the side of the street, or with a cup in front of them begging for money. When something becomes "normal" for us we can become desensitized to it. We tend to tune out all things that do not affect us personally. We are selfish people all caught up in our own lives, and we especially ignore those things that make us uncomfortable.

Until recently, I was one of these people, and then I met Ann. One day during a youth group meeting at my church, Our Lady of Greenwood, I met Ann, an adult of the group. We had been talking about a variety of issues when I mentioned homelessness, and that was when Ann stepped forward. She explained to me how she never told anyone that she was homeless and was in fact living out of her car, though she had attempted to appear as if she wasn't: "It can be very difficult. I often tried to hide that

I was homeless and made my friends think I wasn't." She also explained that shelters were challenging because some required people to be there before nine in the evening and leave by six in the morning, which made it difficult if they were working a night job. As she was talking to me it was hard to fathom because I'd never had to experience homelessness, and this was someone I knew but was never aware of it.

Many people don't understand the reason behind homelessness. Often people's first thought when they see a homeless person, is that this person has somehow brought this on themselves. In some cases, this may be true, but not always. We all judge, even me and my family. When discussing the subject with my younger sister, she blurted, "It most likely had to do with drugs," as to why people found themselves homeless. At the time I agreed with her, but then I slowly started to see every homeless person as a drug addict. Though drugs and alcohol contribute to the majority of homeless people, being at 64% as of March 2021, there are people on the street for different reasons (Murray). Whether it be because they were evicted from their homes, or ran away because of physical or mental abuse, many of these individuals are teens age twelve to seventeen, but drugs are a problem for children as well. Sadly, "71% of missing, runaway, throwaway, or abducted children reported a substance abuse disorder" (Murray). There are also those who are born on the streets that never have known a different life. And now, financial complications due to COVID are becoming more of an issue, with "one expert estimating that nearly 250,000 new people could join this already growing [homeless] population" and that "200,000 remain unsheltered" (Moses). Whatever the case, people should not have to suffer when we, as a country, have so much.

The solution to homelessness is simple; build homes. This idea has been put into action by many organizations, such as Partners in Housing here in Indianapolis and Habitat for Humanity. In Eugene, Oregon, the people decided to act on the homelessness problem. In Georgia Perry's article, Oregon's Radical Solution to Homelessness: A Bare-Bones Shed Village, she tells of Oregon's solution to homelessness by building houses. "They built small wooden sleeping units measuring either 8-by-8 feet or 8-by-10 feet" (Perry). What better way than to literally build them a home? Bring the tiny homes idea to Indy, and start literally building houses for those who need them. The Tiny Home Solution works because it immediately gets a person sheltered and a place for them to call home. Though it is a temporary condition, it gives them a bit more time to get back on their feet. Some might pose the argument that the Tiny Home Solution does not help homeless families with multiple members, and while this is a drawback, if all the single people are in a Tiny Home then the shelters are able to be open for the families and focus on them. When a person is able to call something their own, they are more likely to take care of it and work harder to keep it. Because there are so few consequences to this solution, it is a great way to go.

Better food pantries is another way to go. Recently, I have been helping more with my local food pantry. I talked to my pastor about working toward building a home that might provide relief for a homeless family. I started to get a mission trip to different parts of the US with my friends. I also took an initiative with my close community. The churches around us have always been there and many have extensive resources. The Archdioceses of Indianapolis have a program called the Holy Family Shelter, it "provides housing and supportive social services to homeless families once they have moved out of the emergency shelter" ("Homeless Family Shelter"). People know what to do to help, but though this is a good start, the problem is worldwide, since it is such a major issue we must not stop at our own community.

Everyone has problems to face and their first thoughts might not be of others, but everyone needs to join in the fight against homelessness. Stop focusing on self and think of those who are in need. We need to understand what is happening before we decide to pass judgement. It can be difficult to know who is homeless and in need of help. Like Ann, some people are too ashamed to come out and say that they are homeless. Shame should not be an obstacle for them because the shame is given solely from the people with homes. Instead of giving the impression of shame, they must be given the reassurance of trust and respect. What happens is up to us to decide. Never forget: understanding their situations is the first step.

Works Cited

"Holy Family Shelter." *Archdiocese of Indianapolis,* www.archindy.org/cc/holyfamily/transitional.html.

Moses, Joy. "COVID-19 and the State of Homelessness." *National Alliance to End Homelessness,* https://endhomelessness.org/covid-19-and-the-state-of-homelessness/. 19 May 2020. Accessed 29 Oct. 2020.

Murray, Krystina. "The Connection Between Homelessness and Addiction." *AddictionCenter.com,* https://www.addictioncenter.com/addiction/homelessness/. 24 March 2021. Accessed 31 Oct. 2020.

Perry, Georgia. "Eugene, Oregon's Radical Solution to Homelessness: A Bare-Bones Shed Village." *CityLab,* www.bloomberg.com/news/articles/2014-11-11/eugene-oregon-s-radical-solution-to-homelessness-a-bare-bones-shed-village. 11 Nov. 2014. Accessed 29 Oct. 2020.

Jessica Moran

The Future Is Ours to Write

In life, many of us aspire to make a difference in the world we live in. We look at the issues that have impacted us and the world and try to create solutions. This year has already proven to be one like no other. Constant challenges that the world faces require faster working solutions. However, solutions take time and teamwork to create. These issues are not small things that just impact a few people, they impact the entire world. For example, racism and inequality are issues that have been plaguing many lives for centuries. Our own Declaration of Independence states, "We hold these truths to be self-evident, that all men are created equal," which explains that everyone is equal, no matter what. The United States of America was built on the fundamentals of Natural Rights. Everyone is born with a set of rights which cannot be taken from them. And yet, to this day, many encounter others who try and take away these rights. As a nation, and as a world, we are better than that. Solutions are vital for these issues. As we have seen, the COVID-19 pandemic has also taken the world by storm. This issue has hit close to home for me personally. I never thought that anything could impact my life so much in such a small period of time. The COVID-19 pandemic has truly impacted my life and my thoughts for the future, and it has granted me new insight on what changes should be made in order to benefit our world.

I remember the day when I first heard about the Coronavirus. I was in Spanish class and someone said that three people in China had contracted this virus. Everyone was so naive and thought that it was just a little disease and it might not even get to the US. We were very wrong. Soon, the virus had entered America and was spreading fast. On Friday, March 12th we were sent home from my school for what was supposed to be a two-week shutdown. I was excited at first, because who doesn't like a two-week break? Little did I know that the two-week break would be turned into a four-month quarantine. School eventually went fully virtual and extracurriculars were cancelled. As a student, I was confused at first, just as many were at the time. I didn't know what e-learning would be like. Most of the time it felt as if I was teaching myself, but I knew that this was also hard for the teachers. Some days were better than others. I tried my best to stay positive, but it was difficult. Watching the news and seeing how things were getting worse didn't help either.

As for my family, they were struggling as well. Both of my parents work for different pharmaceutical companies. My mom was lucky enough to be able to work from home. However, my dad was a deemed an "essential employee" and had to still go into work. Every day he would put himself at risk of getting the virus, and every day we would stay home and worry for his well-being. My younger sister was in 5th grade, so she was learning how to do e-learning as well. The days seemed to blend together. We weren't able to go anywhere or do anything fun. No going to the movies. No going to restaurants. No museums. No sporting events. Just constant fear and stress consuming our lives. The entire community was in a state of panic for weeks. Businesses were being closed and many were losing their jobs. Our state government would put out new weekly rules to abide by, as the federal government worked out solutions for the future. After those months of quarantine, the world has never seemed the same. Nothing is the same, and quite honestly, it may never be the same again. The COVID-19 pandemic truly took over my life, the lives of my family members, and the lives of the community.

These past months have truly influenced the thoughts for my future. When I think about my future career, I know that it has to involve helping others. For the past few years, I have been interested in becoming a biochemist. Biochemists help develop new medicines to fight diseases and work in research studies related to these new medicines. During this pandemic, it has become clearer to me that there will always be the need for people who can help develop medicines. Scientists around the world have been working on a vaccine for COVID-19. Without the help of so many researchers, the idea of a future vaccine wouldn't be possible. In those four months of quarantine, I became more aware and soon realized that future problems are likely to arise and possibly cause separation from others. With that realization, I needed to cherish each moment I had with someone. The pandemic has influenced my thoughts for my family in the future as well. My family has always cared about everyone's wellbeing and making sure everyone is safe. In the future, I will be the one caring for my parents and for my own family. I have growing concerns about future issues that will possibly impact my family.

Although no one knows what these issues will be, I will always do what I can to protect my family, myself, and others. If this pandemic has taught me one thing, it's that everyone has to do their part for the well-being of the entire world. This is especially true in order to benefit our world in the future.

The COVID-19 pandemic has given me new insight on what changes I would like to see in the future. In the future, I would like to see a more inclusive group of people who help stop global issues before they get too out of hand. The COVID Task Force has been helpful during the pandemic, but I would like to see more task forces that help resolve different issues. We can look back on problems that took place within the COVID Task Force and revise them for future groups. I would also like to change how children can get a more effective education if they are not able to attend school. Public schools should be given more resources that benefit both the student and the teachers. Right now, schools are doing the best they can under these circumstances. However, teachers were given a task that many have never been able to practice before, which puts them under a lot of stress. E-learning and being at school are two totally different teaching environments. This means that many teachers are having to try different educational techniques to help their students learn. If schools in the future could provide teachers with instructional information on how to teach remotely, it would benefit the students and the teachers. We can use the experiences from students and teachers to help develop future resources for potential online education. The most important change that I want to see in the future is for each person to be positive citizens in the world. We can benefit our communities by being helpful individuals who can work together. As Americans, our country was founded under the idea of Republicanism. This is the idea that individual citizenship helps benefit the country as a whole. By becoming positive citizens, we can help our communities flourish. This goes for everyone in the world as well. In the future, we can all work together to help benefit our world. Change has to start somewhere, and that somewhere is within ourselves. For myself, I have to become the change that I want to see in the world.

The Power of Youth in Our Communities

In today's world, there are many challenges to face, but some of them affect minorities the most. Racism is one of the biggest challenges that concern me and my community. I have witnessed my friends fear for their lives when we're just out at a school event. These concerns have become larger as racism increases in the world. With recent incidents calling attention to this nation falling into a state of pandemonium regarding race, it becomes apparent that the future of our society relies heavily on the youth. Not only should racism be acknowledged, but it should also resonate within society because of the members it has lost due to racism.

It started with George Floyd. He was a forty-six-year-old African American man who was killed in Minneapolis, Minnesota while being arrested for allegedly using a counterfeit bill. Floyd complained about not being able to breathe due to Derek Chauvin, a white police officer, kneeling on his neck for several minutes, but Chauvin did not get off until told to do so by paramedics. But why didn't he just get off when Floyd complained about not being able to breathe? Did Floyd's voice not matter? Did his life not matter?

This event was so unfortunate, but a huge, long overdue wake up call for our world. Now, my community is standing up and demanding justice. At my school, a group of African American students have come together with the idea of forming a group of young activists that will use their voice where there is injustice. The motivation is to raise awareness about Black lives and the way they are being treated by a society with the "white standard." Everyone should understand their voice matters and they should use it even when they're too afraid to. Silence is worse than speaking up while being afraid. Many people rioted, others went out to protest peacefully, but it wasn't enough. There is still no justice.

Then, a new name came about. Breonna Taylor was a twenty-six-year-old Black woman who was fatally shot at her own home by a white police officer. She did not receive justice because the police had a search warrant to go into her home. But was a search warrant the cost of her life? We, as a community, as minorities, are hungry for justice and freedom to determine our own destiny. We don't want to fear going out and getting shot by the police because of our race. We want to live without having to be degraded for who we are. We cannot change where we come from or what we look like, but we can build our character. Martin Luther King Jr. wrote the "I Have a Dream" speech, and in it he said, "I have a dream that my four little children will one day live in a nation where they will not be judged by the color of their skin but by the content of their character." We all have dreams. As a shared community, we dream that there will come a day where everyone is treated as an equal despite their race and isn't judged by the color of their skin, but for who they really are.

One of our nation's founding ideals was that of natural rights. Everyone has the right to "life, liberty, and property" according to John Locke. These are considered natural rights because you are deserving of them as a human being no matter what your race or background is. This idea has been addressed many times on documents like the Declaration of Independence, where Thomas Jefferson stated, "We hold these truths to be self-evident, that all men are created equal, that they are endowed by their Creator with certain unalienable Rights, that among these are Life, Liberty and the pursuit of Happiness." He is basically saying that it should be very clear that we are all created equal. Therefore, we have the same "natural" rights that cannot be denied or taken away by anyone, or at least shouldn't be. We all have the right to live in peace and be free.

The United States is known as the Dream Land, where everything is possible and all about union. We cannot live up to this definition as long as we deal with racism and inequality within our communities. I believe that for a better future, we need to continue standing up and using our voices where there is injustice. We should never stop or give up because there's no change. We have to believe that there will be change as long as there's someone willing to continue fighting.

Nowadays, the biggest movement is "Black Lives Matter." There is an argument that "All Lives Matter," but all lives cannot matter until Black lives do. We all have to face racism as we are facing the COVID-19 pandemic. Not everyone wants to wear a face mask, but most of us still do it because we want our world to get better. It should be the same with the Black Lives Matter movement. We should all work together in the small ways that can make a big difference, like reaching out to others who are a part of a minority group and providing the help they might need. This could also mean we go to different schools and speak on our experiences with racism as minorities. We need to inform and educate people, let it be known that enough is enough. We, as youth, are the future and we will make a change in our world, starting within our communities.

Works Cited

King, Martin Luther. "I Have a Dream by Martin Luther King, Jr; August 28, 1963." The Avalon Project, Yale Law School. Web.

Locke, John, and Thomas Preston Peardon. "The Second Treatise of Government." Upper Saddle River, NJ: Prentice Hall, 1997. Print.

Thomas Jefferson, et al, July 4, Copy of Declaration of Independence. -07-04, 1776. Manuscript/Mixed Material. Retrieved from the Library of Congress.

Society and Acceptance: Out and Proud

There are rainbows in the sky, acceptance in our hearts, and our minds are calm and tranquil. People are going about their days confident, happy, and content. Everyone is comfortable sharing who their favorite characters are in TV shows and movies. A world filled with people who are considerate, kind, and open-minded—and we do not have to be far from that goal, from that ideal reality. Many LGBTQ people live and work in environments where they are not accepted and cared for by their families and society. They are taught that they are unnatural, hated, or damaged, and can be cast aside by those who once promised to love them. Such tragedies occur often and can lead to more pain and suffering, but together, we can bring healing and love. By spreading love, acceptance, and education, we can end the stigma, ignorance, and hate toward LGBTQ people for being their most authentic selves. Together, we can create a community where everyone can be who they are and love openly.

Social media is an effective method to communicate with the masses and to encourage action and unity. Influencers and actors have the following and platform to share their views on society and acceptance, and many will listen and trust the information they share. It is our duty as members of humankind to reach out to these people and encourage and ask them to spread the message of love. To ask them to use their platform and fame to raise the voices of those oppressed by society. Still, social media use is never limited to those with large followings. Everyone can share information regarding the injustices LGBTQ people face and how to help and be a supportive and compassionate human being. Everyone can amplify the voices of LGBTQ artists, writers, and musicians, so everyone's story can be heard and shared. With each message of hope, love, and respect, we can break the barriers between society and LGBTQ people. Together, we can share acceptance to open the minds of all to a world filled with marvelous people.

Accurate media representation of LGBTQ people is vital to creating a society where acceptance and respect are the status quo. People argue that the young generations are more impressionable and will fall trap to the "gay agenda." They believe that the media representation of people who love and live in nontraditional ways will hurt the minds and souls of their children, but they are mistaken. By representing people of all races, genders, sexualities, body types, disabilities, and more in children's media, we allow children to learn how to be empathetic and kind. Children have role models that they can look to who will help them understand how to navigate relationships with other people and to discover their identity. It is difficult to know who you are if there are no ways to describe how you feel, and it hurts even more if there is no one who can relate. It creates a feeling of isolation and distance between oneself and others.

There are shows for children, such as *She-Ra and the Princess of Power* and *The Owl House*, that depict relationships and identities that stray from society's idea of normal. *She-Ra* takes pride in representing characters who love and exist openly as themselves. Two loveable dads make a double dad joke and riddle for their son. Two wives fight to protect each other and others they love. A shape-shifting nonbinary character adds tension and drama to the environment and plot. *She-Ra* shows these people to its audience while never pointing out that there are gay couples or nonbinary people as if they were different, because they are not. *She-Ra* and the way it represents people is in a candid manner, where someone's gender or sexuality is always respected and not made into a character's entire personality. *The Owl House* depicts a young witchling who is scared of being rejected by the young human witch-in-training. The audience witnesses the relationship development between the witchling and human and the tension of a one-sided crush. This show allows people, especially young people, to understand that developing feelings for anyone, no matter their gender, is natural and normal. By exposing children to people who love openly and without fear, *The Owl House* helps them to understand that they can be accepting and loving to those around them. Writers, designers, and artists must continue to represent and include diverse LGBTQ people in the media they distribute. Together, we can create a society where LGBTQ communities and voices are raised and respected by all.

Education is the foundation for creating a society where people are helpful, thoughtful, and respectful. Current education systems fail to teach about LGBTQ events, people, and topics, even if they are relevant to the discussion and curriculum. LGBTQ youth grow up believing that there is no one else like them; that they are different, strange, and unusual. By implementing school programs and introducing LGBTQ topics into the curriculum, teachers can help children learn how to be more accepting and compassionate individuals. Children who learn that LGBTQ people are normal people who love and live as they do, and that they are not creatures to be disposed of, can anchor themselves to these beliefs and are likely to share them with others. Early and continuous education also aids in the development of LGBTQ youth, for they feel the warmth of acceptance and love from their community, even if they do not know they need it yet.

Together, by creating plans to implement diversity that amplifies the voices of the oppressed, we can produce a society that enables people to be authentic and joyful. By sharing our stories and pride on social media, and by representing the LGBTQ community in the media, we can normalize and destigmatize aspects of the LGBTQ community. By educating people about LGBTQ topics and issues, we can amplify the voices of the oppressed and allow for necessary development to occur. Together, we can create a world where people can love whom they please. Together, we can create a world where people can be their genuine selves without fear. Through education and representation, LGBTQ stories and voices can be heard, allowing love and acceptance to spread.

Works Cited

Stephenson, Noelle. "She-Ra and the Princesses of Power." *Netflix Official Site*, 13 Nov. 2018, www.netflix.com/Title/ 80179762.

Terrace, Dena. "The Owl House TV Show." *Disneynow.com*, 2020, disneynow.com/shows/the-owl-house/.

ABOUT FRATERNITAS PRESS

Fraternitas Press is a student-led publisher sponsored by the Department of English at Marian University. Our goals as editors are to encourage creativity and celebrate the spirit of our community. *The Future is Ours to Write* is our second released book. The Fraternitas Press Editors of this collection were the members of the Spring 2021 Line Editing Class at Marian University: Andrea Skirvin, Chloe Ulmer, Erik Hvidston, Jack Adams, Joshua Parrott, and Sarah Snider.

Lightning Source UK Ltd.
Milton Keynes UK
UKHW020654040621
384928UK00011B/895